Brooklyn
NETS

BY JIM GIGLIOTTI

Published by The Child's World®
1980 Lookout Drive • Mankato, MN 56003-1705
800-599-READ • www.childsworld.com

ISBN 9781503824461
LCCN 2018964194

Printed in the United States of America
PA02416

ABOUT THE AUTHOR

Jim Gigliotti has worked for the University of Southern California's athletic department, the Los Angeles Dodgers, and the National Football League. He is now an author who has written more than 100 books, mostly for young readers, on a variety of topics.

TABLE OF CONTENTS

GO, NETS!

In their early years, the Nets were two-time champions of the American Basketball Association (ABA). Then they joined the NBA in 1976. They were one of the NBA's best teams in the early 2000s. The team fell on hard times in recent years. Today, it has a solid group of young stars. Nets fans believe those players are really good. That could mean better times are right around the corner.

5

Joe Johnson was one of the Nets star players in 2013, when the team moved to Brooklyn.

Brooklyn faces off against Philadelphia in this meeting of Atlantic Division teams.

WHO ARE THE NETS?

The Nets play in the Atlantic Division. That division is part of the NBA's Eastern Conference. The other teams in the Atlantic Division are the Boston Celtics, the New York Knicks, the Philadelphia 76ers, and the Toronto Raptors. The Nets have played in the Atlantic Division ever since they joined the NBA in 1976. They have won the division four times.

WHERE THEY CAME FROM

The Nets began play in 1967 as the New Jersey Americans. In 1968, the Americans moved to New York. They became the Nets. The team picked that name because it rhymes with Jets and Mets! Those are two other pro teams that play in New York. Of course, basketball teams *use* nets, too. The Nets moved to New Jersey in 1977. In 2012, they went back to New York as the Brooklyn Nets. Brooklyn is one of five **boroughs** in New York City.

Darryl Dawkins starred for the New Jersey Nets from 1982 to 1987. He was a great shot blocker.

It's New York vs. New York when the Nets take on the Knicks.

The Nets play 82 games each season. They play 41 games at home and 41 on the road. They play four games against the other teams in their division. When the Nets and New York Knicks play, it's called "The Battle of the Boroughs"! The Nets also play 36 games against other Eastern Conference teams. Finally, the Nets play each of the teams in the Western Conference twice. The winners of the Western and Eastern Conference play each other in the NBA Finals in June.

WHERE THEY PLAY

The Nets play their home games at the Barclays Center in Brooklyn. They moved around a lot in their early years. The team's first **arena** was an **armory** in Teaneck, New Jersey. The Nets had six more homes before moving to their current arena in the 2012 season. Many fans take the train or the bus. A station is right next to the Barclays Center.

The huge Barclays Center scoreboard hangs over the Nets' home court.

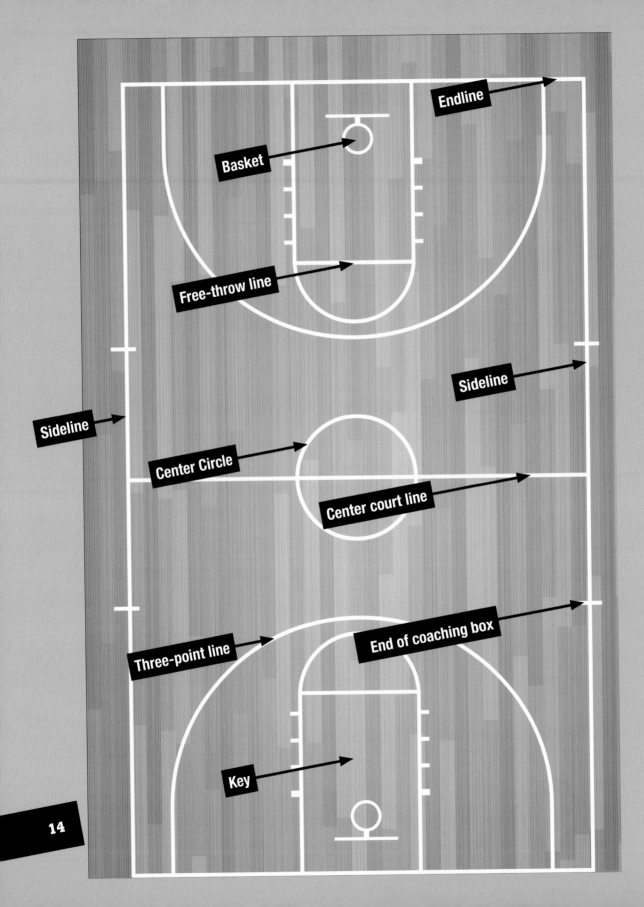

Endline

Basket

Free-throw line

Sideline

Sideline

Center Circle

Center court line

Three-point line

End of coaching box

Key

THE BASKETBALL COURT

An NBA court is 94 feet long and 50 feet wide (28.6 m by 15.24 m). Nearly all the courts are made from hard maple wood. Rubber mats under the wood help make the floor springy. Each team paints the court with its logo and colors. Lines on the court show the players where to take shots. The diagram on the left shows the important parts of the NBA court.

The first event at the Barclays Center was a concert by the rapper Jay-Z. He was a part-owner of the Nets.

GOOD TIMES

Forward Julius Erving led the team to the ABA title twice. The second time was in 1976. That was the last year of the ABA. The Nets and several other ABA teams joined the NBA the next year. The Nets' best stretch in the NBA started in 2002. They made the playoffs six seasons in a row. They won their division four times in those years.

The high-flying skills of Julius Erving thrilled Nets fans. He dunked for the Nets from 1973–76.

The Nets' Devin Harris couldn't get past Orlando's big Dwight Howard. Things like this happened to the Nets a lot in 2010!

TOUGH TIMES

The Nets only won 22 games in 1977, their first year in the NBA. The Nets didn't have a winning season until 1982. Things were bad again in the 1990s. One player wrote "Please" on his right shoe. He wrote "Trade Me" on his left shoe. The worst, however, came in 2010. The Nets started 0–18 that year. They finished 12–70.

ALL THE RIGHT MOVES

Forward Rick Barry was the Nets' first star. He had a **unique** way to shoot free throws. He shot them underhand. It worked. He hardly ever missed. Julius Erving made amazing dunks. He soared through the air. It looked like he could fly! Current star D'Angelo Russell has a great **crossover** move. He changes speed. He changes direction. He leaves his opponent in the dust.

Players shoot free throws after some fouls. The player who is fouled gets to shoot from the free-throw line. Each made free throw is one point.

D'Angelo Russell shows off his dribbling skills. He uses moves like these to get past defenders.

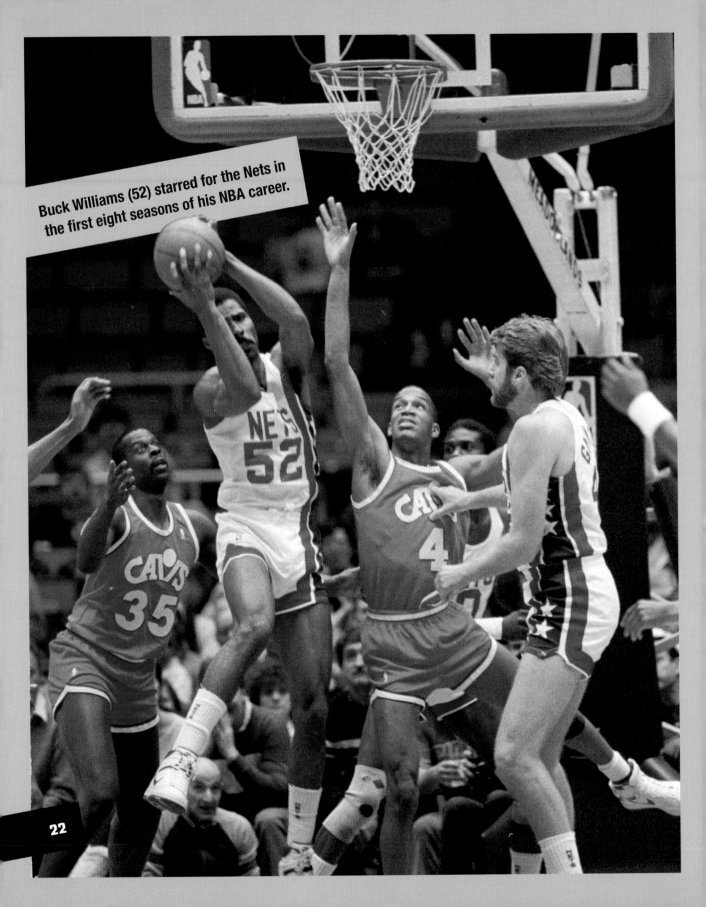

Buck Williams (52) starred for the Nets in the first eight seasons of his NBA career.

Julius Erving was called "Dr. J." He was one of basketball's all-time greats. Jason Kidd played several seasons for the Nets in the 2000s. He was a great **playmaker**. His passing made all his teammates better. Buck Williams played the most games for the Nets. He grabbed the most rebounds. Brook Lopez scored the most points. He passed Williams in 2017. He did it in his last game for the team.

Caris LeVert was a good player his first two years in the NBA. In 2019, he became a great one. He can pour in lots of points. He can pass the ball, too. **Center** Jarrett Allen was a first-round **draft** pick in 2017. The Nets expect big things from the big man. The Nets traded for **point guard** D'Angelo Russell in 2017. He's another young player the team is counting on.

The Nets rely on big Jarrett Allen to battle under the basket with tall stars like Anthony Davis of the Pelicans.

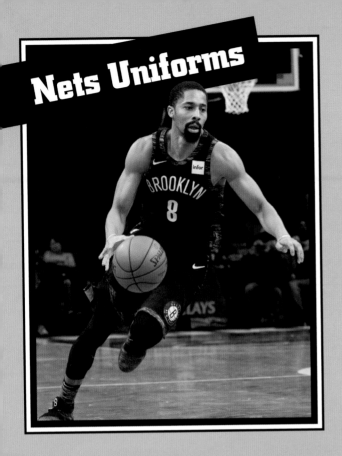

WHAT THEY WEAR

NBA players wear a **tank top** jersey. Players wear team shorts. Each player can choose his own sneakers. Some players also wear knee pads or wrist guards.

Each NBA team has more than one jersey style. The pictures at left show some of the Nets' jerseys.

The NBA basketball is 29.5 inches (75 cm) around. It is covered with leather. The leather has small bumps called pebbles.

The pebbles on a basketball help players grip it.

TEAM STATS

Here are some of the all-time career records for the Brooklyn Nets. These stats are complete through all of the 2018–19 NBA regular season.

GAMES

Buck Williams	635
Brook Lopez	562

POINTS PER GAME

Rick Barry	30.6
Julius Erving	28.2

ASSISTS PER GAME

Jason Kidd	9.1
Stephon Marbury	8.1

REBOUNDS PER GAME

Buck Williams	11.9
Billy Paultz	11.2

STEALS PER GAME

Micheal Ray Richardson	2.7
Eddie Jordan	2.5

FREE-THROW PCT.

Mike Newlin	.886
Jarrett Jack	.885

JASON KIDD

THREE-POINT FIELD GOALS

Jason Kidd	813
Kerry Kittles	687

GLOSSARY

arena *(uh-REE-nuh)* the building in which a basketball team plays its games

armory *(ARM-uh-ree)* a building for housing military equipment

boroughs *(BURR-ohs)* the five different parts of New York City

center *(SEN-ter)* a basketball position that plays near the basket

crossover *(KROSS-oh-ver)* a type of dribble in which the ball goes from one hand to the other

draft *(DRAFT)* the annual event at which NBA teams choose new players

playmaker *(PLAY-may-kurr)* the player who leads a basketball team on the court

point guard *(POYNT GARD)* a basketball player who most often dribbles and passes the ball

tank top *(TANK TOP)* a style of shirt that has straps over the shoulders and no sleeves

unique *(you-NEEK)* one of a kind

IN THE LIBRARY

Doeden, Matt. *The NBA Playoffs: In Pursuit of Basketball Glory.* Minneapolis, MN: Millbrook Press, 2019.

Schaller, Bob with Coach Dave Harnish. *The Everything Kids' Basketball Book (3rd Edition).* Avon, MA: Adams Media, 2017.

Wyner, Zach. *Brooklyn Nets (On the Hardwood).* Minneapolis, MN: MVP Books, 2013.

ON THE WEB

Visit our website for links about the Brooklyn Nets:
childsworld.com/links

Note to Parents, Teachers, and Librarians: We routinely verify our Web links to make sure they are safe and active sites. So encourage your readers to check them out!

INDEX